The Limits of Keynesianism

Dominic Alexander

COUNTERFIRE

The Limits of Keynesianism

First published in Great Britain in 2018 by Counterfire,
Bow House, 157 Bow Road, London E3 2SE.
Cover design and layout: Feyzi Ismail

ISBN 978-1-907899-06-5

A catalogue record for this book is available from the British
Library.

Printed and bound in Great Britain.

www.counterfire.org

Contents

Part One:
John Maynard Keynes and orthodox economics

Economics as a profession was profoundly embarrassed by the financial crisis of 2008, and its standing has been further diminished by the ongoing new 'Long Depression',[1] which was unforeseen by its orthodox practitioners. Demands for a widening of perspectives and approaches in the profession have not, as yet, made for noticeable breakthroughs in elite thinking about alternatives to the neoliberal model of capitalism.[2] As Larry Elliott in *The Guardian* argued:

> *Since the financial crisis broke 10 years ago, policymakers have viewed the disruption as a temporary phenomenon. Growth would pick up. Productivity would rise. Inflationary pressure would increase. Interest rates would return to more normal levels. It hasn't happened.*[3]

The impasse in economic theory and practice today is not unlike that of over eighty years ago when capitalism went into its last great crisis. This was what came to be called the Great Depression, taking over the moniker for the earlier depression of the late nineteenth century, which then became known instead as the Long Depression.

These periodic great crises, and other problematic periods, such as the 'stagflation' of the 1970s, go against one of economics' most cherished orthodoxies, that capitalism in its purity is a stable system. As long as there are not any outside de-stabilising influences, such as government intervention, then capitalist markets will 'return to equilibrium'. It was this assumption that informed the American President Hoover in the early 1930s, famous for the emergence of 'Hoovervilles', mass encampments of the unemployed, under his watch. It is perhaps the memory of the disaster of the 1930s which led US governments after 2008 to pursue mildly reflationary policies (at least in comparison to the British Tories' insistence on uncompromising austerity). The very vocabulary which is now used to describe a government which intervenes to boost the economy during a downturn, goes back to the new economic theory which emerged from the Great Depression, that of John Maynard Keynes.

J.M. Keynes himself came of age as an economist in the period after 'neoclassical economics' was born at the end of the nineteenth century. Although Keynes and Keynesianism are often seen as the opposite of the neoclassical school of economics, his thinking grew out of precisely that context. In the period after World War Two, forms of Keynesian policy became the standard repertoire of governments to manage their economies up to at least the late 1970s. A variant Keynesianism returned after 2008 with such policies as 'quantitative easing'. In the 1960s, it was reported that even Milton Friedmann had said that 'we are all Keynesians now', although he himself claimed to have been somewhat misquoted. Nonetheless, the sheer currency of the phrase is a good indication of the status Keynes had at the time.

Marginalism: aquatic economists
Despite this history, Keynesianism has never dominated the profession of economics, which has remained focused on marginalist theory. The concept of 'marginal utility' emerged in the second half of the nineteenth century, developed by William Jevons among others. While its elaboration is often described as the 'marginalist revolution', it has not generally impressed Marxists

with the profundity of its insights into the nature of the capitalist economy. Very simply, it posits that the value of a commodity to the consumer depends upon the quantity already possessed, so that the additional ('marginal') value of the acquisition of each additional unit will decline in a quantifiable manner. This reflects back on the producer who has to consider the marginal efficiency of capital in investing in each additional unit of production.

This conceptual move was important because it allowed economics to become a highly technical endeavour, where sophisticated statistical applications could dominate the research agenda. Simply applying precise numbers to the abstract marginal values allows all sorts of hypothetical as well as empirical calculations to replace the more problematic analysis of value carried out by the classical economists. If this seems like an unwarranted assault on the integrity of a profession, then consider what an eminent economist himself has to say about the state of his profession in the years before the great crash of 2008.

James K. Galbraith (son of the famous American liberal economist John Kenneth Galbraith), sees academic economics as so dominated by mathematical modelling, proceeding from the concept of marginal utility, that all practitioners of discipline can be divided into 'freshwater economists' and 'saltwater economists'. Both of these groups of economists use mathematical models to prove their propositions, but the latter sort allows a modicum of 'salt', that is to say, messy reality, into their equations, while the former prefers to keep their calculations pure:

> *Economists using mathematical expressions to decorate arguments about the perfection of market systems may believe that their work is beautiful… The main purpose of the math is not to clarify, or to charm, but to intimidate. And the tactic is effective. An idea that would come across as simpleminded in English can be made "impressive looking" with a sufficient*

string of Greek symbols. A complaint about the argument can be deflected, most easily, on the ground that the complainer must not understand the math.[4]

Here, James Galbraith is also unpicking a fundamental tenet of the profession, which is the commitment to the 'dynamic stochastic general equilibrium approach'. This mouthful concerns the assumptions economists make in order to predict economic developments through manageable sets of calculations. Boiled down, it requires that in their models, all actors are identical, and all behave 'rationally' with perfect access to information about the market. Thus:

the economy can be modelled as though there were just one person in it, predicting the future with foresight based on an accurate model, as much calculating power as required, and subject only to random (hence unpredictable) shocks and errors.[5]

A consequence of this approach is that any crisis in the system cannot be due to anything inherent in the nature of capitalism, or 'the market', but must be a meaningless accident, and so, if left alone, the market will restore itself to equilibrium. A major follower of Keynes, Hyman Minsky, is said to have rejected neoclassical economics because 'in its core models, a depression is an impossibility.'[6] The intellectual desert of this kind of thinking does mean that it is difficult for its inhabitants to conceive of alternative ways of thinking, even when confronted with the reality of an ongoing worldwide economic crisis. It seems that little has been learned since Hoover's time after all.

Nonetheless, marginalism has continued to perform another valuable service to bourgeois economics ever since the nineteenth century, and this was to enable it to escape the increasingly intractable problems of classical political economics. Marx was the culmination of that tradition, and working on the basis of bourgeois political economists, most notably David Ricardo, he showed that capitalism was inherently prone to crisis, and riven with dangerous contradictions. The 'marginalist revolution' was the basis for neoclassical economists to be able to declare that Marx was old-fashioned, outdated, and dismissible. Marginal utility theory was, however, just an evasion of the issues. It did nothing to answer any of the problems raised by Marx's analysis. Even so, there was now a new way to approach economics, so old concerns could be dismissed out of hand.

The failure of equilibrium

Events were soon to disturb the complacency of economists, with the disruption of the First World War, and, for Europe in the 1920s, the uncertain recovery from that cataclysm, soon overtaken by the crash of 1929 and the Great Depression. Keynes' economic thinking took place in this context, with the added concern of Britain's evident decline from world power status, giving way to the new strength and dynamism of the United States.

His first notable contribution was 'The Economic Consequences of the Peace', in which he attempted to warn against the harsh peace imposed on Germany by the Versailles Treaty. He pointed out that attempting to extract huge money payments from Germany, reparations, would not be possible unless Germany's exports increased commensurately to provide the requisite foreign currency. This could only occur at the expense of the other power's exports, so they would not be gaining anything.[7] Later, he would criticise Britain's decision to attempt to retain the gold standard for sterling, showing again a willingness to criticise standard thinking, with a particular focus on monetary issues.

It was not, however, until the impact of the Great Depression had worked itself through his thinking that Keynes made really major contributions to economics. His new thinking culminated in the work the *General Theory of Employment, Interest and Money*. It is still debated how far this new theory challenged existing economics, with some Keynesians wanting to claim that his arguments were compatible with orthodox assumptions. However that may be, the key advance of Keynes' *General Theory* was to disprove the old assumption that the market would always return to an equilibrium of full employment. Keynes argued that, in fact, capitalism could come to an equilibrium with high unemployment, and relatively low investment and usage of existing productive forces. Capitalism under *laissez-faire* conditions could no longer be assumed to deliver the best results for society.

In addition to that argument, Keynes did also break to some extent with the methodological individualism of orthodox economics. With the thrift paradox, for example, he showed how a virtue at the individual level could become a social ill. For an individual to save is an act of prudent restraint, but too much saving in the economy overall will lead to a decline in consumption, or effective demand, and this will lead to a decline in production, and then higher unemployment. Aggregated thrift becomes harmful to the economy.

One of the central experiences of the Depression was explained by this insight. The classical argument, that a fall in wages increases employment since the marginal cost of labour becomes cheaper, turned out not to hold true. In fact, the imposition of austerity during a downturn only accentuates economic decline. Keynes pointed out that the argument from a part to the whole, or from the individual perspective to the totality, is absolutely flawed. Thus, in this case, the classical argument ran that if a factory cuts the wages of its workers, it will be able to sell its product more cheaply. Thus, larger quantities will be sold, and the factory will be able to employ more workers.[8]

This will hold true of an individual producer assuming that the wages of *other* workers in the economy are not also reduced. However, the flaw in the classical argument was, and is, precisely to scale up from the individual to the general, without considering that different dynamics govern the different levels of analysis. Thus, at a general level, if firms reduce the wages of their workers, then the total aggregate demand in society will fall, *reducing* demand for everyone's products.

This is a lesson that needs to be applied generally in the analysis of capitalism, and even of societies across the board. Actions that may have a certain logic at the level of individual behaviour, have very different effects at the level of the totality. It is an important aspect of Keynes' economic thinking that he was able to perceive this problem, which is referred to as the 'fallacy of composition'.[9] Indeed, it leads to important policy prescriptions at the heart of the Keynesian response to the Great Depression: do not react to a downturn with cuts in government spending.

In response to collapsing aggregate demand in the economy, the state must absolutely not respond to the fall in its own income (through the fall in tax receipts, as economic activity collapses) with austerity. The effect of fiscal austerity will be a severe deepening of recession, as Germany found to disastrous cost in the early 1930s. Rather, the state must spend money to stimulate demand; only state spending can lift the economy out of the downward spiral. Declining demand leads to collapsing production, which raises unemployment, leading to even less demand, and so on. Prudent economic behaviour at the level of the household precisely does not scale up to the level of the state.

If the 'fallacy of composition' is a key insight of Keynes, it remains only a partial one. Keynes did not go on to examine capitalism in a fully dialectical way, grasping the contradictory dynamics of the parts and the whole, as Marx had done before him. Rather, Keynes remained wedded to an essentially empirical 'common sense' approach, in which the simple relations of 'supply and demand' remained his essential analytical tool. The result is an impressive, indeed crucial system of economic analysis and policy, but a contradictory one also.

Keynesianism can be both highly critical of capitalism, and yet committed to maintaining it. It contains essential insights which can lead to important reforms within the system to the benefit of working people, and yet elements which encode a surrender to the interests of capital at crucial moments. Picking apart these elements of Keynesianism requires an extended discussion of its theory and application since the 1930s, before a balanced assessment can be made of its use to the greater project of the emancipation of labour.

Part Two: The assumptions of Keynesianism

Keynes could be dismissive of the inheritance of classical political economy precisely because its concerns had been largely bypassed, and marvelled that Marxism should be 'a portent to historians of opinion – how a doctrine so illogical and dull can have exercised so powerful and enduring an influence over the minds of men'.[10] This comment is from an essay of 1926, which might be considered a minor piece. Yet, sometimes theorists are more revealing about the basis of their thinking in their occasional writing than in their major works.

Here, despite the Russian Revolution, Keynes was still seeing Marx and Marxism as something that clearly belonged to the past, to outdated thinking. That he grasped nothing of the challenge Marx's analysis offered to economics is further made clear by his astonishing claim in another essay that the rejection of 'the Benthamite calculus', made by him and his contemporaries, protected them from 'the final *reductio ad absurdum* of Benthamism known as Marxism'.[11]

The Benthamite calculus was that of the utilitarian philosopher, Jeremy Bentham (1748-1832). It was a kind of rationalism which attempted to apply the principle that everything can be reduced to a calculation of the relative pain or pleasure caused to a given number of people by a particular action. Everything should be judged according to that measure. Among the rational calculations to which this philosophy gave rise was the idea that if you deprived the poor and unemployed of any support except the most miserable possible conditions in a workhouse, then they would be inspired to find suitable work to support themselves. The rational application of pain thus would result in the greater happiness for the whole of society.

In order to draw a line between Bentham and Marx (he does not explain it any further in the passage quoted from above), Keynes must be reasoning from the assumption that Marxism takes economics, in a reductive way, as the foundation of society. Keynes is here revealing his own assumptions about economics, and not Marx's. In Keynes' reading, Marxism must assume that everyone is only motivated by immediate selfish individual interest. That would be true of Bentham and other bourgeois thinkers of his time, but is certainly *not* of Marx, whose analysis begins at the social level, not with the selfishness or otherwise of individual human actors. The comparison with Bentham reveals, therefore, that the only Marxism with which Keynes could have had any acquaintance, before the First World War, would have been particularly vulgar versions of Second International Marxism. It seems also that no events thereafter opened Keynes' eyes to the real nature of Marxist theory.

The larger topic of this essay, in which he accuses Marx of Benthamism, was concerned with ethics and rational individualism, in a discussion that is more allusive than precise. Nonetheless, it is revealing as the older Keynes is reflecting on the assumptions with which his younger self embarked on his career. It uncovers the underlying reasons for the limitations of Keynes' economic theory. Although in insights like the 'fallacy of composition', he was able to challenge the conclusions of orthodox economics, he never fundamentally departed from the standard assumptions of methodological individualism at the heart of orthodox economic analysis.

Keynes' aggregate fails to reach Marx's totality

Keynes' central concepts of aggregate and 'effective' demand, that is the anticipated quantity of demand in society as a whole (combining investment and consumer demand), do start from a collective standpoint rather than the perspective of individual consumers or producers.[12] As Michael Roberts says, this 'meant that the fluctuations in a capitalist economy could be considered in their whole and not just ignored or dismissed.'[13] Robert Skidelsky, the economic historian and biographer of Keynes, agrees about the latter's 'rejection of methodological individualism as a generally valid method of analysis in economics'. He further claims that there was a vestige of Hegelianism in Keynes' thinking, due to his acceptance of the idea of organic unity; that is to say, that with a whole consisting of interacting parts, 'its value – as in a work of art – can be greater or smaller than the sum of those parts.'[14] This vestige seems to make little appearance in Keynes thinking, however, other than in this one essay on his early beliefs.

If Keynes had fully abandoned methodological individualism, he ought to have been in a much better position to understand the underpinnings of Marx's thinking, and could not have seriously dismissed Marxism as ultra-Benthamism. Despite his grasp of the different dynamics at the levels of individual behaviour and the collective, Keynes never mounted a systematic critique of preceding political economy or his contemporary economics. Rather, he suggested limited revisions of it, leaving certain methodological assumptions in place, and so avoiding a confrontation with some of the difficult questions about the nature of the capitalist system.

This evasion seems to explain some of the philosophical meandering in which he engages in the 'Early Beliefs' essay. He avers that he and his contemporaries were more influenced by an 'English puritan tradition' concerned with 'the intimate connection between "being good" and "doing good"', which provided 'a purer, sweeter air by far than Freud cum Marx.'[15] In essence, what Keynes was doing in this philosophical memoir was to outline an ethical idealism 'joined with the unsurpassable individualism of our philosophy' which lay in contrast with 'the Benthamite calculus, based on an over-valuation of the economic criterion.'[16]

This individualism enabled Keynes' circle to be the 'last of the Utopians... who believe in a continuing moral progress by virtue of which the human race already consists of reliable, rational, decent people.'[17] Keynes goes on to criticise the over estimation of the rationality of human nature in his early thinking, but in doing so is not suggesting a change of perspective, from the individualist to the social, as an approach which would better take into account the complex reality of human social relations. Instead, he is simply adding a somewhat resigned complication to the assumption that a rational economic individual exists as the foundation stone of economic analysis.

This digression into philosophical issues reveals certain evasions in Keynes' thinking which ultimately have important consequences for his economic models. The rejection of Marx and Freud, under the cover of criticism of Bentham, a figure of much less significance, amount to a disavowal of the attempt to understand the hidden structures of human social life. Where Marx argued that attempts to change the world need to be based on an analysis of the real tendencies and contradictions of society, Keynes is suggesting an ethical 'utopianism' divorced from an 'overestimation of the economic'. Rather than address the failures of neoclassical economics to understand capitalism as it actually is, Keynes preferred to move the discussion over to a supposedly separate ethical sphere.

Again, the charge against Marxism, via Benthamism, is hidden away, but does concern this apparent distinction between 'ethical' and 'economic' behaviour. If behaviour is rationally economic in a restricted sense, then it is selfish rather than ethical. Marx argues that society is driven by class relations, therefore, according to Keynes, Marx must mean that individuals are only capable of class-based selfish behaviour. This is, of course, to understand class through a methodological individualism; as if class were a personal characteristic rather than a social structure in which individuals are embedded and constrained to act in certain ways in order to survive.

Keynes' assumption that this entails a non-ethical standpoint certainly shows that he could not have read Marx at all seriously, given that his moral outrage in *Capital* is plain to see. However, it also highlights the strictly limited way in which Keynes transcended 'methodological individualism' in his theory of aggregate demand; the later concept does not in fact amount to an analysis starting from the point of view of society as a whole. Rather, it and the allied concept of 'effective demand', are both based simply on the agglomeration, or summation, of expectations about individual consumers' demand. Aggregate demand is, in fact, no more and no less than the sum of its parts, rather than opening up to view the hidden workings of a system conceived as a totality. Keynes could not grasp the importance of Marxist economic theory, because he could not, or would not, accept its social premise.

Keynes, Malthus and common sense

The limited rejection of methodological individualism seems to go hand in hand with Keynes' preferences in the classical tradition. He rejects Ricardo in favour of Malthus. In Ricardo, bourgeois political economics accepted a labour theory of value, and was beginning to perceive intractable problems in the nature of capitalism, including the tendency for the rate of profit to fall. The analysis of these problems would be developed and corrected by Marx, which was reason enough for bourgeois economics to abandon classical political economy altogether. Keynes contrasts Ricardo's systematic attempts to analyse production with Malthus' 'common-sense' approach where:

> prices and profits are primarily determined by something which he described, though none too clearly, as "effective demand". Ricardo favoured a much more rigid approach, went behind "effective demand" to the underlying conditions of money on the one hand and real costs and the real division of the product on the other hand, conceived these fundamental factors as automatically working themselves out in a unique and unequivocal way, and looked on Malthus's method as very superficial. But Ricardo, in the course of simplifying the many successive stages of his highly abstract argument, departed … away from the actual facts; whereas Malthus … had a firmer hold on what may be expected to happen in the real world. … When one has painfully escaped from the intellectual domination of [Ricardo's] pseudo-arithmetical doctrines, one is able, perhaps for the first time for a hundred years, to comprehend the real significance of the vaguer intuitions of Malthus.[18]

This is a remarkable passage in the way it charts a path for Keynes away from the problems of classical political economy. It provides him with an intellectual tradition to justify a dogmatically superficial empiricism in which only the immediate appearances accessible to 'common sense' are worthy of attention. Ricardo's attempts (Marx is probably the real intellectual target here) to access the hidden mechanisms of capitalist relations are dismissible as a wasted hundred years. As David Harvey comments on opponents of the labour theory of value:

> *Physical materialism, particularly in its empiricist garb, tends not to recognise things or processes that cannot be physically documented and directly measured.*[19]

Keynes and his followers were dismissive of the concept of value in economic theory because it could not be perceived directly by empirical observation, and yet, as are many non-material phenomena, it is real. It is particularly in the study of human society that immaterial relations, such as value, class, status or solidarity, need to be grasped as real forces. The refusal to go beyond 'common sense' lies behind Keynes' failure to overcome methodological individualism beyond a superficial level. He could not pursue an economic analysis that would lead into the intricacies of capitalism's inner workings. This would take him beyond the concept of the aggregate of demand into a more dialectical understanding of the dynamic social relations which drive capitalism, and indeed any type of economy.

Keynes' choice of Malthus as an intellectual progenitor is a curious one in some respects. Keynes evidently wished to escape the world of Ricardo and Marx, where the necessity of class antagonism could not be avoided. Yet, it is not immediately obvious how Keynes and Malthus can be reconciled. Malthus is, of course, famous for his doctrine of population, that human numbers will always increase at a faster pace than agriculture's ability to produce food. Malthus' most notorious passage is that concerning a man who is born without the means of subsistence:

> and if society do not want his labour, has no claim of right to the smallest portion of food, and, in fact, has no business to be where he is. At nature's mighty feast there is no vacant corner for him. She tells him to be gone, and will quickly execute her own orders, if he do not work upon the compassion of some of her guests. If these guests get up and make room for him, other intruders immediately appear demanding the same favour.[20]

All this, and more, Keynes quotes without apparent disquiet, as an anticipation of his own theory of effective demand. This is despite the fact that a century of unprecedented population growth had disproved Malthus' central hypothesis. Instead, Keynes seeks to turn Malthus inside out; instead of demand exceeding supply, in Keynes' theory of 'effective demand', it is the existence of consumer demand which drives investment into the expansion of production. It is true that in Malthus there is a defence of the existence of the rentier aristocracy, as their luxury consumption produces employment for those workers who would otherwise be banished from nature's feast as excess population.[21]

Yet, Keynes was also famous for claiming that the rentier class either should or would be wholly extinguished by the development of capitalism.[22] Effective demand, in Keynes, comes more efficiently from the general population than from a small rentier class' luxury consumption. Given all this, it is hard to see why Keynes would want to claim Malthus as an ancestor. The connection, however, is in the simplicity of Malthus' approach to economics. Avoiding all discussion of the nature of production, of the origins of value and profit, Malthus boils it all down to a very basic theory of supply and demand. This suits Keynes very well as it short-circuits the difficult problems of classical political economy.

Keynes against labour

There is another sting in the tail to this, which is that Malthus' reasoning produces an argument to decry trade-union demands for higher wages: a rise in wages simply leads to higher prices.[23] In fact Keynesians often make the same argument; a sign that despite his reputation as a left-wing figure, Keynes and his theory are by no means always likely to fall on the side of labour against capital.[24] Indeed, even when discussing war profiteers in the famous essay, *The Economic Consequences of the Peace*, Keynes insisted that these were 'the entrepreneur class of capitalists, that is to say, the active and constructive element in the whole capitalist society'.[25] Keynes rejected both David Ricardo's and Marx's labour theory of value, alongside the whole subject of value, so he inevitably saw capital as productive in itself. This presupposition would not dispose him to side with labour as such, even when he clearly moved to the left in the wake of the Great Depression.

If it is apparent that Keynes was temperamentally opposed to dialectical reasoning, it is nonetheless the case that his economic theory was born of a brilliant pragmatism in response to events. Hence his reaction to the Versailles treaty was clear sighted, where the politicians were apparently determined upon an economic revenge in order to justify their persistence in an unprecedentedly murderous war. The vast reparation payments imposed upon Germany were not payable except through an increase in German exports:

> *Germany can pay in the long run in goods, and in goods only, whether those goods are furnished direct to the Allies, or whether they are sold to neutrals and the neutral credits so arising are then made over to the Allies.*[26]

It would also be necessary to factor in the necessary limitations to German imports, requiring 'a regime in which for the future no German drank beer or coffee.'[27] Such austerity would, of course, have a depressing effect upon those economies that might export to Germany. Even if British and French export industries were not directly implicated in this, the knock-on effects would haunt them also. In the end, the full scale of reparations would have to be reduced, and American finances be used to stabilise the German economy after the hyperinflation episode of 1923.

There is, nonetheless, a degree of naivety in Keynes' dissection of the problem; there is a sense that he is accusing the Allied governments of economic illiteracy in their policy. That much might well have been true, but there was a clear line of reasoning in play which Keynes ignored; the logic of power and imperialism. Britain and France decided upon a dangerous *economic* strategy, because it was thought that only the subjugation of Germany could restore the real standing of the former imperialist states. In the end, the plan did not work, at least entirely, and the consequence was the confirmation of the USA's newly leading position as an imperialist power.

Keynes' economic thinking therefore tended to assume an economic sphere that operated in a neutral fashion, free of the effects of social power relations internally, and externally in terms of imperialist competition. Keynes did not recognise class as a structuring force within the domestic economy. Neither did he factor imperial power relations into his consideration of the operation and tendencies of international trade. It needs, therefore, to be borne in mind that Keynesian economic theory, like orthodox economics, operates on a plane abstracted from the real relations of political economy.

Part Three: Marx, Keynes and the analysis of the trade cycle

The assumption of orthodox economics in Keynes' time was that the capitalist economy, despite perturbations, would always return to an equilibrium in which productive capacity is used to its fullest extent, and hence employment is at maximum levels. The worst thing a government could do would be to intervene, as this would only upset the natural recovery of markets to this ideal equilibrium. In the light of the numerous economic crises of the nineteenth century, it is difficult to see how this orthodoxy remained in any way credible. Nonetheless, this doctrine, known as Say's Law, remained accepted within the field of orthodox economics until the Great Depression of the 1930s rendered it unsustainable, as it was shown that an underemployment equilibrium could last at least a decade.[28] This turned out to be only a temporary setback for the law: the long years of neoliberalism have made it, guardedly, acceptable again.[29]

Say's Law had it that supply creates its own demand. If one area of production is overproducing and another underproducing, market action will bring about equilibrium. It can be presented within an apparent common-sense logic of demand and supply to appear plausible, but it only does so in an abstract way, divorced from the real movements of the economy. Marx consistently ridiculed 'the insipidities' of Say, writing, for example:

> In order to prove that capitalist production cannot lead to general crises, all its conditions and distinct forms, all its principles and specific features—in short capitalist production itself—are denied. In fact it is demonstrated that if the capitalist mode of production

had not developed in a specific way and become a unique form of social production, but were a mode of production dating back to the most rudimentary stages, then its peculiar contradictions and conflicts and hence also their eruption in crises would not exist.[30]

Say argued that supply created its own demand, since if a producer made a commodity, then the workers would be paid, and would thus be able to buy the product. On a generalised scale, this would mean that if goods were produced there would be an available demand for them. If one producer was making too much of one commodity, and another too little of a second, then the laws of supply and demand would even that out sooner or later. Equilibrium would be achieved.

For Marx, this would not work, because it ignores the nature of production itself, both the need for capital accumulation and surplus value. At the most basic level, Say's law assumes that all exchanges happen simultaneously, but in reality, this is not so. In fact, if there is too great a gap of time between actions of sale and purchase, then the result is crisis.[31] This is only the beginning of the difficulty. To take another aspect, because the worker does not receive the full value of the productive labour expended, the wages a worker earns are not equivalent to the value of the commodity produced. There is a shortfall, and crisis is therefore endemic to the system. The same dynamic also produces an overaccumulation of capital, with the potential for production being much higher than the capacity to consume. Marx's arguments on this issue were, of course, ignored by orthodox economics.

The uncertainty of animal spirits

Keynes also discarded Say's law, but his reasoning differed from that of Marx. He was not concerned with the inner nature of the production process, and did not consider exploitation as a factor in any way. He reasoned simply from the principle of supply and demand, and retained the basic assumption of Say's Law that a certain quantity of production ought to be matched by equivalent demand. The problem lay, for Keynes, in the motivation for investment and therefore production:

> the act of saving implies, not a substitution for present consumption of some specific additional consumption which requires for its preparation just as much immediate economic activity as would have been required by present consumption equal in value to the sum saved, but a desire for "wealth" as such, that is for a potentiality of consuming an unspecified article at an unspecified time.[32]

In one respect, Keynes comes close here to Marx's formulation of the capitalist cycle as being M-C-M' (capital to commodity to capital plus profit), unlike in pre-capitalist exchange relations where the cycle went C-M-C, as use values rather than exchange values were dominant. The problem with Keynes' conception here is that it does not make any class distinctions between capital and worker, or producer and consumer; the classical assumption that all are equal participants in the market remains unquestioned. This narrowed focus is made easier in Keynes by the absence of value analysis, which in Marx is key to revealing the hidden workings of capitalism.

Nonetheless, the upshot for Keynes is that the cycles of capitalism are affected by the problem of *uncertainty*, which makes investors prefer to hoard or save capital in certain market circumstances. Rather than reaching equilibrium, the fear that an acceptable return on capital will not be made inhibits investment. There is a direct relationship between employment and investment in this argument:

> It follows, therefore, that, given what we shall call the community's propensity to consume, the equilibrium

level of employment, i.e. the level at which there is no inducement to employers as a whole either to expand or to contract employment, will depend on the amount of current investment.[33]

Investment depends upon an estimation of likely consumption, but this is inevitably guesswork, and so depends ultimately on the sheer mood of the economic actors. Hence the often quoted concept of the 'animal spirits' of investors, which Keynes invoked to explain the problem:

Enterprise only pretends to itself to be mainly actuated by the statements in its own prospectus, however candid and sincere. Only a little more than an expedition to the South Pole, is it based on an exact calculation of benefits to come. Thus if the animal spirits are dimmed and the spontaneous optimism falters, leaving us to depend on nothing but a mathematical expectation, enterprise will fade and die; - though fears of loss may have a basis no more reasonable than hopes of profit had before.[34]

If capitalists are not confident that they will receive an acceptable return on the capital they advance, then they will not invest the capital, but prefer to keep it as cash or savings. This problem is known as the liquidity trap. The result is that workers are not employed, and do not earn wages. Effective demand then is reduced, and commodities are not bought. An economic downturn follows as a consequence, but it is not the outcome of a real crisis of profits; it is not rooted in exploitation, or the cycle of value, but in the *confidence* of capitalists. It is a psychological problem, rather than one rooted in the value cycles of production and circulation.

Investment does not rest purely on confidence, of course. In discussing the marginal efficiency of capital, Keynes outlines how inducement to invest depends partly on the investment demand schedule and partly on the rate of interest.[35] The demand schedule involves the cost involved in producing 'an additional unit of such assets', that is to say output, which can vary greatly depending upon the nature of the commodity in question. And yet, Keynes warns, the marginal efficiency of capital 'is here defined in terms of the *expectation* of yield and of the *current* [original emphases] supply price of the capital-asset.'[36] Once again, the subjective view of the capitalist becomes centre-stage. The other side of the equation, the disincentive to invest, depends upon the rate of interest, but that is no more objective a factor: 'It is evident, then, that the rate of interest is a highly psychological phenomenon.'[37]

State investment, wages and inflation

Keynes worked out his *General Theory* as an answer to the obviously defunct classical theory that capitalism will always return to full employment in a state of equilibrium. He reduced the problem to one of investment; only if investment is high enough will production be at a level which can produce full employment. Yet, investment depends upon the interest rate, which 'in convention is thought to be rooted in objective grounds', but which Keynes showed was subjective. There was hope, he thought, in the fact that 'precisely because the convention [about long-term rates of interest] is not rooted in secure knowledge, it will not be always resistant to a modest measure of persistence and consistency by the monetary authority.'[38]

This is Keynes' justification of government interference in the market to stimulate demand; if interest rates are subjective rather than objective by nature, then there can be no technical objection by economists to the adjustment of the stimulus to investment by an actor 'outside' the market. Indeed, as Skidelsky comments, the upshot of the analysis of the marginal efficiency of capital and its relation to interest rates is that 'only an exogenous injection of demand can get the economy moving again' once it has sunk into low confidence and therefore depression.[39]

This hopeful conclusion is undermined as the analysis goes on, as even with a stimulus to investment confidence, there are many factors which will kick in to reduce the marginal efficiency of capital, and confidence in further rounds of investment. The monetary authority will be limited by its wariness of incurring debts, and low interest rates can themselves induce people to hold cash instead: 'In this event the monetary authority would have lost effective control over the rate of interest.'[40]

Even where intervention is successful in reflating the economy, 'as soon as output has increased sufficiently to begin to reach "bottle-necks", there is likely to be a sharp rise in the price of certain commodities.' This then reduces effective demand, or puts pressure on wages to rise in response to rising prices. The result is that 'the wage-unit may tend to rise before full employment has been reached.'[41] In one respect, this appears to be critical of capitalism, in that Keynes is positing that full employment is unlikely in normal circumstances.

However, there is a sting in the tail for labour here. The analysis produces a justification for the classic ploy to divide workers against each other; the employed are being selfish in asking for higher wages, because that will prevent the unemployed from finding jobs. Labour is caught out both ways, and a healthy economy depends upon workers restraining their wage demands. Otherwise that delicate flower, the confidence of the capitalist in his profits, will be damaged, to the detriment of all. Indeed, Keynes' close ally, Joan Robinson, identified trade unions' level of ability to bargain for higher wages as a key element in what leads to a crash during a period of high employment.[42] In this respect, Keynes, far from being the economist for society, even less for the cause of labour, cleaves strongly to the interest of capital. It could not be otherwise, when his analysis always starts from the perspective of capital in regard to the whole economic process.

Keynes is led in this direction as there is, in fact, a lacuna at the heart of his whole analysis. The theory provides no material analysis for why confidence, and therefore investment, should rise and fall, short of the tautology that during a boom, confidence leads to overinvestment, which then turns into the flight to liquidity when confidence declines. What is missing is, of course, the analysis of profitability in terms of the production process that Marx provided.

It is important to analyse the circulation of value, but this must be rooted in an understanding of the structure of production.[43] Keynes' implicit argument against concerning oneself with the dynamics of production, is the principle of uncertainty, and that therefore there are no 'scientific' processes going on beneath the realm of the circulation of commodities. However, it is not necessary to assume the neoclassical myth of total market knowledge on the part of every actor, to posit that capitalists are aware of the likely rate of profit for any investment, and that decisions are made accordingly. The analysis can assume a social average, where the vicissitudes of individual decision making are ironed out, in order to assess the objective processes governing production. Thus, if there is a problem with investment, leading to a systemic crisis, this, in the Marxist view, will be due to material problems in the economy, rather than purely psychological ones.

It is important to bear in mind these differences in approach, so as not to be misled by the superficial similarity between Keynes' theory and one aspect of Marx's analysis. Keynes posits that there is a permanent tendency for capitalism to develop the problem of a lack of effective demand. This can be compared to the underconsumptionist reading of Marx, where productive capacity is not matched by the workers' ability to consume the products of their labour.

The gap between the two theories is the absence of an analysis of class and exploitation in Keynes. Where in Marx, the problem is inescapable, and is one of the drivers of the tendency to crisis, in Keynes the problem is contingent on the balance of investment confidence. It can, provisionally, be fixed so that capitalism could achieve a long-term, even permanent, stability. The problem then becomes one of attempting to encourage investment by various inducements. Uncertainty and speculation become the central determinant of the analysis of trade cycles, rather than any material problems with the nature of capitalist production.

The financialisation of theory

In the absence of a theory of value with which to analyse the circuits of capital, and the relations between production, distribution and exchange, Keynesianism tends to be driven to explain phenomena through a psychologising subjectivism. Hence Keynes himself could only analyse the realm of finance and credit in these terms:

> *Americans are apt to be unduly interested in discovering what average opinion believes average opinion to be; and this national weakness finds its nemesis in the stock market… Speculators may do no harm as bubbles on a steady stream of enterprise. But the position is serious when enterprise becomes the bubble on a whirlpool of speculation. When the capital development of a country becomes the by-product of the activities of a casino, the job is likely to be ill-done… These tendencies are a scarcely avoidable outcome of our having successfully organised "liquid" investment markets.*[44]

It is notable here that there is no explanation of the circumstances in which 'speculation' dominates 'entrepreneurs', or when the latter are able to hold the former in check. The issue is, of course, very complex and difficult within Marx's analysis, but value theory offers a way of understanding the dynamics involved with credit and speculation. The tendency within Keynesianism is to ignore the ways in which different circuits are connected, as for example the 'rootedness of credit in commodity money' which has 'been informally bypassed by Keynesian policies after the 1930s'. [45]

After Keynes, this tendency to deflect analysis towards the psychological was only increased. This is so even among left-leaning Keynesians, whose attention is increasingly drawn away from what is sometimes called the 'real economy', towards the sphere of finance, taken as essentially separate, but determining the former. It is true that there is a long-term tendency for capitalism to develop an ever-greater financial sector as opposed to the directly productive sphere, and that this tendency is especially marked in the decades after the 1960s.

Unlike Keynes, Marx's analysis of value is able to open several windows on tendencies of the credit system and its relation to the production and circulation of commodities. Credit, not merely 'speculation' in Keynes' terms, is both necessary to the circulation of capital, but also produces unstable forms of fictitious capital. [46] The increasing 'financialisation' of economics is also partly explained through the rising organic composition of capital. Where the increase in the use of technology reduces the share of labour in production, it therefore reduces the relative quantities of surplus value being produced. Since labour is the only source of value, as the technological input into production increases, the rate of profit will therefore decline.

This is to say, there is an increasing mass of capital seeking areas in which to invest, but, irrationally from the point of view of the system as a whole, it does not necessarily invest itself in surplus-value producing activity. The result is that capital will turn away from production towards speculative activity in the hope of capturing a greater rate of surplus value. This result is a parallel to Keynes 'liquidity trap' theory, but explains the reasons for the process, where Keynesianism merely suggests the ebb and flow of confidence.

The financialisation of Keynesian theory reached its

peak with Hyman Minsky, for whom economics could concentrate entirely on the financial sphere. Indeed, Minsky drew out the theme in Keynes' theory that depressions were caused by speculative bubbles themselves; the 2008 crash is sometimes referred to as a 'Minsky moment'. This makes the capitalist market flawed in the sense that it is driven by irrational dynamics, but, equally, it means that capitalism does not have the internal contradictions that Marx saw, by which it would tend towards self-destruction. Rather, it would respond to the regulation of speculation alone.

Minsky added an analysis of the role of debt in the capitalist economy to Keynes' understanding of investment confidence and speculation. As Steve Keen describes it, the business cycle begins with the economy in a state where growth is enough to reduce unemployment, but where firms and banks are both conservative in their willingness to invest or lend. However, this results in a situation where 'most projects succeed', and therefore:

> Investment projects are evaluated using less conservative estimates of prospective cash flows, so that with these rising expectations go rising investment and asset prices.[47]

The result is that caution is abandoned and both firms and banks take on more debt, credit increases, the economy moves into a 'euphoric' stage, and 'Ponzi' financiers come into the equation. Thus, a bubble is soon created, which will necessarily burst due to the pressures generated within the system, leading to a collapse of investment and a depression.[48]

In this view, recession and depression are generated by the internal cycles of finance itself, not for any other contradictions within capitalism. The implication here is that crises can be controlled or even largely prevented by the actions of monetary authorities; in short capitalism can be saved from itself, and has no long-term tendencies towards an increasing magnitude of crisis.

Keynes himself argued that booms 'are almost always due to tardy or inadequate action by the banking system'.[49] Slumps, in this argument 'may sometimes get out of hand and defy all normal methods of control', but that would require therefore more extensive government intervention than the 'normal' policies. The upshot is that crisis is amenable to moderation, at least. For Minsky the role of crises is in fact to strengthen capitalism.[50] Nonetheless, the reason mainstream economists tend to ignore or dismiss Minsky is made clear by his judgment about capitalism; 'Not only is stability an unattainable goal; whenever something approaching stability is achieved, destabilizing processes are set off.'[51]

Euthanasia of the rentier
Keynes' solution to the tendency of capitalism towards instability was the idea of socialising investment; or the 'euthanasia of the rentier'.[52] This was a response to his concern that 'the richer the community, the wider the gap between its actual and its potential production', as capital will find it difficult to find sufficient investment opportunities. As a result, 'the more obvious and outrageous [will be] the defect of the economic system.' Superficially, Keynes appears to approach Marx's analysis of the falling rate of profit here, but the mechanism is wholly different:

> *For a poor community will be prone to consume by far the greater part of its output, so that a very modest measure of investment will be sufficient to provide full employment; whereas a wealthy community will have to discover much ampler opportunities for investment if the saving propensities of its wealthier members are to be compatible with the employment of its poorer members.*[53]

This is the operation of the liquidity trap, and suggests

to Keynes that society would demand an end to the system as a result of the widening gap between potential and actual prosperity.

Keynes thought this was realistic on the grounds that as the economy developed, accumulation would mean that capital would become more abundant, and according to the laws of supply and demand, this would mean that it would become cheaper. And yet, despite the massive quantities of capital accumulated since Keynes' time, we do not live in a world where the 'rentier' faces extinction. Part of the reason for this is that the system does not actually operate according to simple laws of supply and demand, but through the value cycle of capital, where profit is the overriding driver of all processes. There are also problems with Keynes' simple concepts of interest and money, and indeed 'rentiers', but these also relate to his rejection of value theory.

The problem with explanations based on laws of supply and demand, according to Marx, is that at equilibrium, supply and demand cease to explain anything.[54] That is to say that 'fluctuations in the reciprocal relation between demand and supply can merely explain deviations of price from value, not value itself.'[55] Instead, the value circuits of capital need to be explored. One aspect of the problem is that the overaccumulation of capital leads to crises of profitability. Capital does not become abundantly cheap, but rather demands returns which are increasingly difficult for the social capacity for consumption to provide.

David Harvey analyses the consequences of this, showing that the financialisation of capitalism in recent decades is exactly a function of capital seeking areas where it can command a higher return than from the production of commodities themselves. This means it flows into areas like property speculation, which are parasitic on the productive economy, but where an individual capital can find spectacular rewards. This lasts until the house of cards collapses, as in 2008. Minsky was therefore right to see the tendencies of capitalism to produce Ponzi-scheme moments. However, he was not able to root it in the deeper processes of capital value-circulation, precisely because the Keynesian school rejects value analysis, resting on an abstract supply and demand analysis.

Without an understanding of the processes of value, and the way that value is embedded in precise, historical social relations, Keynesian theory can see flaws in capitalism, but not explain why crises change in nature and impact over time. As a result, capitalism appears fixable in a Keynesian analysis; since the dynamics are conceived in abstract rather than historical terms, they should be amenable to technical adjustments which should balance the system.

There are a range of policies which can be applied to make adjustments to the system. At the conservative end, there is tinkering with interest rates, or capital-friendly quantitative easing, designed to boost the 'confidence' of capital. At the most radical end, there are solutions such as the socialisa-tion of investment, which can have a progressive impact, at least in the short term. Yet, none of these measures take into account capital's uncompromising drive to profit, and the way in which capital will resist any efforts to reduce its share of the return on investment.

Thus, some quasi-Keynesian solutions, such as quanti-tative easing coupled with government austerity policies, actually become a means by which capital attempts to solve a crisis by increasing its share of value at the expense of the rest of society. Such policies make people, that is to say the proletariat (in the most broadly understood sense), pay for the crisis, while protecting profitability as much as possible. The socialisation of finance, for example, which appeared to be a possibility during 2008 as many major banks faced collapse, was not allowed to become a reality. Instead, gov-ernments in most of the developed world socialised the costs of bailing out the banks, while ensuring that these institutions could return to profitability.

The reason why the apparently radical proposal of the 'euthanasia of the rentier', fails to gain purchase, is because of Keynesianism's failure to address social relations of production, and the way in which capital is embedded in a social and political system geared towards the protection of capital's ability to reproduce itself; the process of M-C-M', or profitability. Yet, even so, the proposal is not nearly as radical as it sounds, depending as it does, upon an undialectical separation of production and finance capitalism. The aim, firstly, is not to abolish capitalism, but to preserve it. Secondly, the problem with this procedure is that it is not possible to separate 'good' producer capitalists from 'bad' financial capitalists, as the two functions are, in practice, wholly bound up with each other.[56] It is *not* possible to abolish the problematic parts of capitalism by reigning in or transforming the nature of finance alone; the *whole* system from production to investment needs to be socialised.

Resuscitation of the rentier

These issues are related to another area in which Keynesian theory departs crucially from the Marxist explanation of crisis. Keynesians seek to blame crisis on policy failures, in the regulation of banks and lending, for example, and therefore see the financial system itself to be the direct cause of crises. Marx allowed that this sector could contribute to crisis (in 1847-8 and 1857 for example), but held that finance was not constitutive of crisis in itself.[57] If the 2008 crisis had been merely an issue of policy and regulation of finance, then by now there would have been a genuine recovery. The failure of that to appear points to a much graver malaise in contemporary capitalism.

Keynes' theory is two sided; on the one hand it has a radical aspect, but on the other it is wholly geared towards the encouragement of capital. It takes as a given, rather than as an historically determined phenomenon, that capital is the only social actor which is capable of driving economic activity. This results in at least one argument which carries noxious social implications. Keynes noted the disutility of gold mines, as they add 'nothing whatever to the real wealth of the world', but imagined the government filling 'old bottles with banknotes' then burying them 'at suitable depths in disused coal-mines which are then filled up to the surface with town rubbish'.[58] The government would then lease these mines to private enterprise, which, to get at the money, would employ labour. This would reduce unemployment, and because people would be being paid, due to the 'multiplier effect' of their consequent spending, the economy would grow at a greater rate than the government expenditure entailed.

This scenario is reproduced in real life by quantitative easing, where the government buys its own bonds, thus cheapening credit, and supposedly thereby encouraging investment. The difference is that quantitative easing does not directly create any employment, whereas Keynes' notion of 'digging holes in the ground' would do. Keynes said that it 'would, indeed, be more sensible to build houses and the like; but if there are political and practical difficulties in the way of this, the above would be better than nothing.'[59]

The 'political and practical difficulties' will always set in, however, because of the social power of capital. We have ended up in an even worse situation than Keynes envisaged, where quantitative easing flows to the benefit of capital, and financial speculation makes housing unaffordable. Minsky admits that when 'conservatives are Keynesians, then tax and spending policies may well be used to give life to rentiers rather than to abet their euthanasia.'[60] Far from the euthanasia of the rentier, the 'political and practical difficulties' ensure that only capital's interest is really considered in economic policies.

While left-leaning Keynesian economists would object that the implementation of policies such as quantitative easing are not the right sort of government intervention- ism, there is the bias in the whole theory that whatever stimulates capital is better than nothing. The obverse is that anything which discommodes capital ought necessarily to be restrained or eliminated. This is a political weakness in the logic of the theory as it leads directly to the free-market position that all restraints on capital necessarily harm wealth production, and make everyone poorer.

This problem clearly lies behind the ambivalence among Keynesians about trade unions. Minsky, with apparent approval, quotes Keynes from an essay written in the 1920s, saying that trade unions were 'once the oppressed, now the tyrants, whose selfish and sectional interests need to be bravely opposed.'[61] Keynes thought he had done away with what he saw as the 'muddle' of Marxist economics, and rejected the 'statism and homogeneity' which followed from socialist ideas.[62] The demands that social-democratic governments have constantly made, even before the crises of the 1970s, that workers and trade unions show restraint in their wage demands, flows, in one respect, from the main tendency of Keynesian thinking.

The notorious Labour government white paper, 'In Place of Strife' (1969), which proposed restrictions on trade-union rights, was no accident, nor the simple result of weakness in the face of right-wing forces. The Keynesianism which generally guides social-democracy policy has an internal logic which tends towards the restraint of labour, at least as much as capital. This is even before the institutional power of capital over government is considered as a pressure upon social-democratic governments to 'moderate' their demands on capital.

Part Four: The Keynesian attack on the labour theory of value

In Keynesian thinking, there are arguments in favour of more egalitarian societies, and a preference for higher shares of social wealth to be directed towards the mass of people. Nonetheless, its theory never abandons the perspective of capital. Analytical individualism is so ingrained that even a consciously left-wing Keynesian economist like Joan Robinson misinterprets Marx at several points in her critique, because she assumes the perspective of a single capitalist to be the starting point, where Marx's analysis takes the social whole as prior. Alongside this is the refusal to understand value as a social relation, insisting upon a reductive materialist analysis. With these two prior assumptions at work, Keynesians like Robinson or heterodox economists like Steve Keen leap to dismiss the labour theory of value.

Robinson attacked the very concept of value, arguing that it was just metaphysical, a 'mysterious emanation' in Marxism that 'was still somehow lurking in relative prices'.[63] Yet there is a difference between a quality that cannot be apprehended as a concrete substance and something that has no real existence. There are different analogies that can explain this, but one is human consciousness. So long as we do not invoke Descartes' ghost in the machine, consciousness is a phenomenon of the material world, yet there are no particles of consciousness. It does not exist in this or that neuron as a tangible unit. Rather, it is the creation of the totality of brain *activity*; it is an emergent property that depends upon movement, or process, to come into a very real existence.

Value is very similar, except that it exists at the level of total *social* interactions, rather than neuronal ones. In a parallel way, value can only exist if the volume and complexity of economic interactions reaches a certain level in a society. Thus, in medieval economies the level of exchange was at a relatively low level and intensity (in the sense that production for exchange represented a low proportion of household activity). While the presumption that labour had something to do with the value of a commodity was present, it was not strong enough as a social relation to overcome other influences on price. Value was not, consequently, a dominant relation over the processes of production.[64]

In a different analogy, David Harvey uses gravity to explain:

> *As such it [value] is, like gravity, an immaterial but objective force. I cannot dissect a shirt and find atoms of value in it any more than I can dissect a stone and find atoms of gravity. Both are immaterial relations that have objective material consequences.*[65]

There are many very real phenomena that cannot be isolated as discrete physical objects, and social relationships are almost a category on their own of these real but 'immaterial' forces; there is no substance in which we could locate love, solidarity, or class conflict.[66] However, if we follow the arguments of economists like Joan Robinson, we should dismiss their existence, since each case is like that of value; 'It has no operational content. It is just a word.'[67]

Marx against reductionism

Dismissals of Marx's labour theory of value often assume his conception to be identical with that of his predecessor, the classical economist David Ricardo (who was no friend of the working class). Marx took Ricardo's theory but altered it in subtle but crucial ways, so these criticisms actually fall at the first hurdle.[68] One type of argument used against the labour theory of value is to take some substance with rarity value and claim that its high price as against other commodities shows that the labour inherent in it cannot therefore be the measure of its value.

One example that has been used by way of illustration is the case of ambergris (whale vomit). A chance find of a pile of ambergris upon the beach can be sold very lucratively to the perfume industry, and yet the person who finds it has expended very little labour, while walking upon the beach, relative to the amount of exchange value involved. The flaw in this reasoning, and many others like it, is that it assumes that value is defined through individual cases. This is not so; value is a *social relationship* and is defined through the social processes involved.

It is not the individual labour in a particular commodity item that is the measure of value, it is the total *socially necessary labour* time that defines the value contained in commodities of a particular kind. It is not one person walking upon a beach, but the average social labour taken. That is to say, what counts is the total hours spent by the total number of people, walking along all the available beaches, that has to occur before one person strikes it lucky. The case of ambergris actually bears out Marx's theory so long as it is read, as it needs to be, in the social frame, not the individual one. As Harvey says:

> Marx defines value as socially necessary labour time. The labour time I spend on making goods for others to buy and use is a social relation.[69]

This is important in a methodological way. It defines the difference between Marx's dialectical version of materialism, and the standard positivist version almost universally espoused in academia:

> Physical materialism, particularly in its empiricist garb, tends not to recognise things or processes that cannot be physically documented and directly measured.[70]

A real science of economics must not take a reductive materialist approach if it is to understand capitalism. Capitalism needs to be seen in terms of a series of social relations which create particular dynamics. Positivists want all facts to lie upon the surface, to be directly observable and countable, and yet, as anyone at all acquainted with modern physics will grasp, reality just does not work like that. What Marx's analysis achieves is to lay bare the often counter-intuitive results of the dynamics of capitalism, which are hidden from plain sight.

For Robinson, wedded to the capitalist's pragmatic perspective, this is precisely what is wrong with the theory of value; it does not correspond to common sense; 'the academics can score a point against Marx, who always reckoned in terms of average cost, because in this connection the principle of marginal cost, or rather cost at the margin, corresponds to common sense.'[71] Yet, Robinson fails to notice that just as common sense does not necessarily correspond to the real workings of the world, the perspective of the individual capitalist does not correspond to the social dynamics of the whole. In this respect, Keynes' thinking was superior to his supposedly more radical ally, as when he was able to perceive the counter-intuitively negative impact of individual saving on the whole economy.[72]

The dynamics of the social whole

So, again, in Marx, value is determined by the social average amount of labour needed to produce a commodity, but how much a capitalist will produce and at what price that commodity will be sold depends upon a range of factors.[73] At a social level, the profit returning upon commodities will be determined by the ratio of labour and capital in their production, which is known as the organic composition of capital (the greater the amount of machinery and other capital investment, the higher is the organic composition). This does *not* mean that a particular factory relying upon more human labour than machinery will receive a higher rate of profit than a technologically more advanced one, even though the former factory is more productive of surplus value than the latter.

This is because the more advanced industries, with a higher organic composition of capital, tend overall to capture a higher share of the socially available surplus.[74] The dynamic of capitalism is contradictory here, with the industries which produce more surplus value capturing less of the socially available surplus than those with a higher organic composition of capital. This is even though the latter, because they use less labour relative to capital, or have a higher labour productivity, produce relatively smaller quantities of surplus value. The tendency over time is therefore, at the social level, for a smaller proportion of value to be produced than capital advanced, leading to a tendency for the rate of profit to fall.

Critics of Marx simply do not follow this line of argument, insisting that the 'facts' must indicate that everything, capital, labour, machinery and raw inputs included, must contribute to value. The failure to accept that the analysis must proceed from the perspective of the social whole is the problem. Robinson, for example, insists on evaluating the concept of value according to whether an individual capitalist can use it to determine the price at which particular commodities should be sold, showing to her satisfaction that a capitalist will not rationally sell commodities on the basis of value, but rather of marginal utility.[75] In arguments such as this, Robinson entirely misses the purpose of Marx's analysis because of the profound methodological differences between her positivist Keynesianism and the dialectical Marxist approach.

Most of Robinson's arguments against Marx founder because she refuses to accept the concept of value according to Marx's usage; the critique therefore only proves Robinson's own assumptions to be erroneous, not Marx's.[76] The degree to which Keynesians tend to import their own assumptions into the discussion of Marx is revealed acutely where

Robinson absurdly claims that Marx's argument depends upon Say's Law at points, when Marx is well-known to have held Say in some contempt.[77]

More fundamentally, Robinson, at the start of her argument on the labour theory of value, refers to labour *time* without clarifying the role of labour *power*. The distinction is absolutely crucial to Marx's revision of Ricardo's version of the theory. Labour *power* is a qualitative term, in which the social relations are revealed; it is the potential for productive power, whose realisation depends upon a struggle between labour and capital over how much value the latter can extract from the former, in return for a given quantity of wages.[78] The difference between labour time and labour power also explains why a machine or an animal cannot be the source of surplus value; both can only release the value embodied in their reproduction, whereas only human labour can, firstly, transform past labour into a new form, and secondly, be made to create more value than is required to reproduce itself.[79]

Reducing Marx

The core of Robinson's critique of Marx's labour theory of value, and Steve Keen's following Robinson, comes down to what is known as the transformation problem.[80] This is a highly technical issue centred on only one section of *Capital*, so it is rather disingenuous of both Robinson and Keen not to acknowledge this.[81] It has been pointed out that this section, even though Engels included it in volume three, was written in 1864/5, before the publication of volume one in 1867.[82] The assumptions made in it cannot, therefore, be taken to represent the entirety of Marx's labour theory of value.

Unfortunately, this is precisely what the Keynesian critics do, holding it as representative of the entire argument. Robinson and Keen claim, on the basis of the passage in volume three, that Marx holds the rate of surplus value to be constant across time and different industries, and apply this to the logic of the whole theory. That, however, is just an analytical limiting assumption made at this particular point in order to make a set of calculations possible.[83] Elsewhere, since the rate of surplus value is a measure of labour productivity, Marx allows it to vary. Any reading of the rest of *Capital* would show Marx's analysis works through the consequences of the variations of the rate of surplus value. Marx's transformation tables in volume three were not meant to do the work that the Keynesians imputed to them, and the critique has therefore been founded on false premises. Whatever the technical problems involved, the issue is certainly not the definitive disproof of the labour theory that Marx's critics have presented it to be.

Robinson insists that Marx's analysis depends upon a constant rate of surplus value in order to debunk the argument about the falling rate of profit.[84] Her discovery of fatal 'inconsistencies' in Marx simply ignores how the analysis is built through holding some factors constant at certain points, in order to explore the resultant dynamics. Re-introducing the held factors then produces a dialectical understanding of the movements of different tendencies. In spite of Robinson's assumption, the impact of a rise in the rate of surplus value has, in fact, contradictory effects.

On the one hand, if new processes or technology make labour more productive, that can cheapen the commodities needed for the reproduction of labour. The resultant lower wage costs can have the outcome of a boost to the rate of profit. However, a generalised raising in the organic composition of capital, also a result of rising labour productivity, will depress the rate of profit. Which tendency within the dialectical movement becomes dominant depends, for example, on the extent of generalisation of new technology through different sectors of industry. Over time, nonetheless, the tendency for the rate of profit to fall is likely to re-assert itself. Robinson's reading of the whole argument insists instead on a one-to-one offset, reducing complex dynamics of real economic relations to an abstract, linear movement up or down in magnitudes.

There is a constant tendency among non-Marxist economists to attempt to reduce the qualitative relations through which Marx analyses the dynamics of capitalism, such as value or labour power, to quantitative measurements. Yet, this is neither the goal of Marx, nor is it the function of the concept of value. Paul Mattick dismissed the 'transformation problem' some time ago explaining that:

> *Of course, the "transformation" is* only a way of saying *that although everything in the exchange process occurs in terms of prices, the latter are nevertheless determined by value relations of which the producers are not aware. This determination of price by value* cannot be established empirically; *it can only be deduced from the fact that all commodities are produced of labour … There is no observable "transformation" of values into prices; and the value concept has meaning only with regard to total social capital.*[85]

Both Robinson and Keen find Marx frustrating and irrelevant because value does not automatically convert to prices. What is the point of an analysis which cannot predict particular prices?[86] A commitment to the reductive materialist outlook is necessary for a capitalist perspective, but that is not the same as it embodying truths about social relations. In fact, Marx's employment of irreducible, qualitative concepts reveals his analysis of capitalism's drive towards alienation as a pervasive and unfolding structure of capitalist social relations. This is the history and the future of capitalism.

By contrast, in Keynes, capitalism has no complex history, only a quantitative, linear trajectory towards an increase in the availability of capital. Shorn of a history embedded in social relations, the abstract capitalism of Keynes' analysis is far more one-dimensional in its dynamics than Marx's. Thus, Keynes expected the increase in capital over time to mean that it would become cheaper, as the ahistorical law of supply and demand would indicate, and therefore society would benefit. Instead, quite different results accrue upon the mounting overproduction of capital in a global economy where the proportion of value being produced is declining relative to capital. The result is an economy where speculative booms and crashes are driving forces, and where the post-war Keynesian consensus broke down in the course of the 1970s.

Real consequences of philosophical differences

The methodological and philosophical differences between Marxism and Keynesianism are not, therefore, just abstract issues, but go to Keynesianism's inability to perceive that all economic questions are really questions about social power. The policy choice that favours capital or labour will not be determined by an objective, rational judgment based on a wider economic good, but on the social power of the two contending camps. The absence of value theory also allows Keynesians to imagine that a balance can be found between the interests of capital and labour. This can lead Keynesians in government to demand sacrifices from labour for the sake of that balance. Value theory allows Marxism to see how crises of profitability have and will lead capital towards the most vicious possible of assaults on labour in order to restore profitability.

None of this means that Keynesian policies are not useful to the working class, or that a reformist government basing its economic programme on some form of Keynesianism should not receive support from the radical left. It does however mean recognising that Keynesian economics of themselves are not likely to lead even to partial victories for labour; the ability of such policies to deliver improvements and ameliorations to capitalism has depended historically on the willingness of capital to make concessions. When conditions have changed for capital, as they did in the 1970s, there have been concerted campaigns from the supporters of capital to shift the burden onto labour.

Keynesianism was thus also unable to deal with the collapse of its standard model in the 1970s, with stagflation leading to a newly determined ruling-class attempt to reverse the gains of post-war reformism. In essence, this was about the crisis of profitability.[87] If then, Keynesianism is a double-edged sword at least, does this mean that the capitalist economy can never be bent towards the interests of the proletariat? The history of labour struggles suggest that what matters is the organised power of the working class.

Part Five: Can the working class make advances within capitalism?

Electing a government which will pursue a Keynesian programme of economic stimulus, instead of austerity for people and public services, can appear as an over-riding goal for the immediate interests of the working class. While such a government would undeniably be preferred, the problems begin precisely at the point where reformist politicians attempt to manage capitalism and an historically capitalist state. Keynesianism is constructed around an intention to stabilise capitalism rather than liberate the working class, and that makes the historically determined requirements of particular ruling classes a priority for any government, left to itself. Keynesian economic policy is therefore part of a broader picture of the reasons why reformist governments tend to fail. And yet, the pursuit of reforms within capitalism is not merely a vain endeavour, and the history of the struggles of the labour movement clarifies how and why this is so.

The principle which dominated policy in the early decades of industrial capitalism was *laissez-faire*, the notion that everyone was best served if there were no limits on the market, and the government restrained itself from intervening. This is the free-market orthodoxy which in various guises has re-appeared in mainstream economics ever since. Of course, *laissez-faire* was never adhered to at all strictly whenever wider capitalist interests required government intervention, not least, for example, in the building of the railways. In Britain, free-market dogma faced a significant defeat almost as soon as the interests of industrialists were given full political recognition through the parliamentary Reform Act of 1832. It was partly in revenge for this political setback that Tory landowners faced down liberal economic orthodoxy to pass the Factory Act of 1833, which made minimal efforts to restrict child labour in certain parts of the textile industry.

The reactionary country party, which the Tories were then, would not have seized on this issue with which to embarrass their liberal opponents, if there had not been already a prominent workers' movement demanding both social and political reform. In various moments, working-class discontent threatened revolutionary consequences, as in the Merthyr Tydfil rising of 1831 or the Chartist inspired General Strike of 1842, to name just two.[88] The Chartist agitation, and the events of 1842 in particular, certainly motivated parliament to pass the Ten Hours Act of 1847, which, while not itself achieving the titular promise, paved the way for a ten-hour day to become the norm not too long afterwards. Piecemeal reforms such as these eventually gave the lie to the plaintive cries of classical economists such as Nassau Senior that restrictions on hours would ruin industry, as all profit was made in the last hour of the day. In so far as breaches in the principle of *laissez-faire* were made in Britain during the nineteenth century, they were driven by the strength of extra-parliamentary workers' movements, and in the teeth of orthodox economic theory.

The first industrial state where a significant advance towards a welfare state was made was also ruled by one of the most reactionary of ruling classes. In the second decade of the newly unified Germany, the 1880s, the chancellor Otto von Bismarck, then the dominant political figure, tried to rally patriotic feeling around the Emperor and cast the socialist movement as a threat to the Reich. A united and formally Marxist workers' party had been founded in 1875, and was rapidly growing in the breadth and depth of its support. Bismarck's attempts to repress it, however, merely strengthened the organisation.

It was clearly in response to this problem that Bismarck introduced a series of social insurance measures, for illness, accidents, and then in 1889, for old age. Britain did not follow suit in this sphere until 1908. Germany was significantly behind Britain in industrial terms during the 1880s, although it was to catch up rapidly thereafter. Nonetheless, the chronology of welfare reforms indicates that it was not economics, but politics, which led the way. Bismarck would not have introduced these measures unless he feared the potential of the growing workers' movement, with its political wing being far in advance of anything in Britain at the time.

The real foundations of the welfare state were put in place in Britain by the radical Liberal government of 1906-14, under pressure from a growing labour movement and the newly formed Labour Party. The significance of this is that the beginnings of the amelioration of capitalism began well before Keynesian economic theory. Indeed, 'Keynesian' economic policies were first employed in Sweden during the 1930s, before Keynes himself had developed justifications for them.[89] The reasons for that lie in the balance of class forces in Sweden at the time. It is therefore the context of class struggles and mass movements through which economic policy can be bent away from the interests of capital, and towards that of labour. Yet, there is no recognition of this pattern in Keynesian theory itself, which is resolutely abstracted from historical social relations.

Reforms and reversals
The high point of reformism in Britain came with the Attlee government of 1945-51, and its signal achievements of National Insurance, a state education system,

the council-housing programme, and above all the National Health Service. These were collectivist policies that derived not from economic theory, but from pressure from below in the labour movement itself:

> *These policies were anathema to the Tory and Liberal parties. They were thrashed out and championed not so much by Labour Party leaders as by rank-and-file members who wanted to change the world in which they worked.*[90]

The Attlee government was far less radical when it came to economic policy, retreating from progressive Keynesian policies rather quickly after some initial signs of boldness. Despite the nationalisations of some industries, which were largely acceptable to capital at the time, the most serious inroad into the autonomy of the market was legislation which enabled the government to step in to 'redistribute and reorganise industry', shifting production to depressed areas.[91] Otherwise, the Labour government quickly bowed to the pressures of economic orthodoxy in the difficult post-war conditions; faced with a balance of payments crisis, the choice was made to impose austerity through cuts in rationing, increases in indirect taxes, and severe wage restraints. And yet, industry was doing well, with production 30% above the level of 1938, while exports had risen 55% above the pre-war level from a very low base, and were the highest in Europe.[92]

These policies were not Keynesian in any sense, being directly deflationary, but do highlight the vulnerability of governments to the pressures of capital. Keynesian theory assumes that the state is neutral, and can intervene in a rational way, above the competing interests of capital and labour. The post-war Attlee government was one of the best opportunities to pursue a radical Keynesian strategy. There was the legacy of war-time planning, at a time when the legitimacy of free-market capitalism was at a particularly low ebb. Additionally, the government had a gigantic parliamentary majority. And yet, a radical, reformist economic policy was not pursued. It should be remembered that Keynesianism itself fundamentally revolves around the confidence of capital, and this was precisely the problem that Labour ministers perceived.

As Tony Cliff put it, even the left-wing Aneurine Bevan 'was anxious to reassure private capitalists that their interests were being looked after, so as to gain financial stability for the economy as a whole.'[93] Even a minister with a pre-war reputation for radical anti-capitalism, Stafford Cripps, as Chancellor 'associated himself with slightly messianic ideas of self-sacrifice and austerity'.[94] As a result, in 1949, the government, in response to the devaluation crisis, and in order to restore capital confidence, removed a host of wartime controls over industry. The Minister responsible, Harold Wilson, according to Paul Foot, 'basked in the praise of Tory MPs, and started to believe that his own political aims were not very different from theirs.'[95] The result of all this was that a demoralised Conservative Party was able to start to regain its sense of confidence and purpose.

The attacks on the working-class standard of living by a reformist government had some serious political consequences for the labour movement as well. The demands of wage restraint sparked opposition that compliant union leaders struggled to contain. The relatively low level of actual strikes was nevertheless met with draconian war-time legislation, such as Order 1305, which made strikes illegal, and even the use of the military for strike breaking. An atmosphere of red-baiting was encouraged by this, the most revered of Labour governments:

> *The minister for labour regularly attributed strikes to Communist agitation. An enormous*

*weight of vilification was heaped on the heads of shop
stewards who during the war had been described as
loyal patriots, but were now "extremists" and "sub-
versives". Labour set the tone for what was to be a
long-running witch-hunt of industrial militants.*[96]

Labour ministers were doing the ideological work of
capital here, and preparing the ground for the return of a
Tory government in 1951. An austerity enforcing, strike
breaking government, which was attempting to tame the
movement which brought it into power, was hardly likely
to maintain the electoral momentum of 1945. Conflict
between the government and rank-and-file trade union-
ists could not have any other result than disorientation
and disillusionment in the movement. The result was
thirteen years of Tory government, before the next,
more technocratic Labour government of Harold Wilson, where the drift away from radicalism was more than
confirmed.

The poison of imperialism

The degree towards which the Attlee government
conformed to the requirements of a capitalist state was
particularly pronounced in the realm of imperialism. A
peacetime conscription policy was introduced for the
first time, and the length of service was maintained at
eighteen months, despite opposition in the parliamentary
Labour Party, because the whole body of the military
leadership threatened to resign if the compromise of
twelve-months service was introduced.[97] Friendship
with apartheid South Africa was maintained for the
sake of the uranium needed for the nuclear-weapons
programme, and for Cold War reasons.[98] Britain played a
vicious and bloody role in restoring colonial possessions
to imperial control, not only for its own, but for French
and Dutch imperialisms as well.[99]

For the Labour government to be accepted as

legitimate, it had to show itself committed both to British capital's own imperialist interests, and to the new post-war hierarchy of imperialism, with the US now firmly in the lead. The American Marshall Aid programme was a powerful instrument in forcing western European states to follow the US lead, and Britain was no exception in this. The end result was Britain's commitment to the Korean War, which required a great expansion in military spending. There was never a question who was going to pay for it; austerity and cuts in public spending ensued, most symbolically with the introduction of charges relating to dentistry and for spectacles.[100]

This was all a far cry from Denis Healey's 1945 commitment to a distinct foreign policy which would 'protect, assist, encourage and aid in every way the Socialist revolution wherever it appears,' and which would avoid Labour 'running with the Red Flag in front of the armoured car of Tory imperialism and counter-revolution.'[101] Yet this is precisely what they did. The realm of the military, war and foreign policy, that is to say imperialism, is not a side-issue for any reformist government, on which it can make compromises in order to further its own economic strategy and goals. The requirements of imperialism directly contradict all progressive economic policy, and impose austerity for the working class, in order to pay for the military needs of capital.

A radical Keynesian policy could not be adopted precisely because of British capital's historical interests and investments. It could be argued in the abstract that capital does not require this imperial dimension. In practice, however, the embedded interests of particular capitals, and institutions like the civil service and the military which exist to defend the interests of capital, will not surrender on these issues merely to an argument from abstract reason. The only power capable of shifting the agenda is the organised force of the working class.

Unfortunately, in the immediate post-war period, the labour movement was largely entwined with and committed to a Labour leadership, which soon turned against its interests in so many ways.

The permanent arms economy

In fact, the whole post-war period, which is often vaguely remembered as a golden-age of Keynesianism, was nothing of the sort. What drove the Western economies was not a radical policy devoted to planned investment in the social good and expanded consumption, but a military Keynesianism which prioritised capital-intensive arms spending. Military spending did act as a stimulus to the economy, and even Ronald Reagan can be considered a kind of 'Keynesian' in that respect.[102] Galbraith emphasised the cost to the American economy of the emphasis on military production from the start of the post-war period, with such expenditures being 'approximately 26.5% of all federal government expenditure', alongside the share in employment with 'as much as a third of all American engineering and scientific talent' employed for military purposes.[103]

This contrasts with Germany and Japan, whose restricted military spending meant that they 'were clear economic beneficiaries of their own defeat'.[104] This is true, but only through a narrow view, a point of which Galbraith ought to have been well aware, as the success of the German and Japanese export regimes depended upon the draw of US markets in particular. German post-war economic recovery had a great deal to do with the demand created by the Korean War in particular. Effectively, in this analysis, Galbraith was acknowledging the phenomenon that some Marxists started calling the 'permanent arms economy' in the 1960s.

The problem which underpins the drive towards this, and away from a more socially productive form of Keynesianism, is historically complex, but one crucial aspect is the overaccumulation of capital. With increasing quantities of capital seeking profitable investment, capital does not become cheaper with less leverage upon society, as Keynes had envisaged. Instead, because capital is embedded in institutions and social power, it is able to distort economies towards its own interests; imperialism is a necessary means of controlling access to opportunities for the reproduction and accumulation of capital. It is also a powerful means of destroying, or at least subordinating, rival capitals.

Moreover, military spending is an ideal form of investment in a situation where capital has over-accumulated 'for it has involved a systematic destruction of values, not a relocation of their use, and it has acted in integrating the system far more effectively than any other form of expenditure.'[105] Keynesians cannot just wish away this drive within post-war capitalism. The end of the Cold War only underlined the centrality of arms spending, since far from there being a 'peace dividend' as many expected, spending on the military in the US remained as great as it ever had been.

Keynesian reforms and the class struggle

There could therefore be an argument, following Galbraith, that Keynesianism in its true form has not been tested and found wanting, but that it has never been tried. The reasons for that however lie in the weaknesses of the theory. The crisis of the 1970s, where standard Keynesian demand management broke down in the face of the new phenomenon of 'stagflation', or simultaneous rising prices and low growth, was at base a problem of the falling rate of profit.

Keynesian theory never really explained the problem of stagflation, or the reasons for the shift in elite thinking towards neoliberalism by the end of the 1970s. Galbraith, for example, simply nods towards the context of the international economy reducing the space for demand management.[106] The freedom of capital under 'globalisation' certainly provides the mechanisms by which national governments can be disciplined by capital, but does not explain why elite interests were so determined to drive this process forward; it was indeed partly a political agenda. Keynesian theory neither addresses the fundamental and complex drives within capital accumulation, nor does it allow that economic policy is subject to the balance of forces in the class struggle.

Should Keynesianism therefore be rejected altogether by those who wish a radical transformation of society? After all, it could also be questioned whether reformist governments are necessary. It is true that post-war West Germany, France and even Spain developed more generous welfare regimes than Britain without social-democratic governments.[107] Certainly, it is important not to underestimate what can be achieved even without reformist electoral victories, but social-democratic governments do achieve important advances, despite their inherent limitations.

The Attlee government created the NHS, which no Tory government would have done. Other state health programmes are fundamentally insurance systems, whereas the original NHS structure was based on collective provision through central funding out of state taxation. That it emerged from the socialist movement, and was driven by rank-and-file activists, rather than the Labour Party leadership as such, is also crucial to an understanding of the role of reformist government. The latter opens a window, but the strength and assertiveness of social movements are essential to real victories.

There is a danger also on the other side, that an absolute rejection of Keynesian policy can lead revolutionaries into a sectarian cul-de-sac. It can be argued that since the cause of capitalist crisis comes down to the problem of profitability, then there is no solution to crisis short of revolution. This kind of argument can risk aligning Marxists with a right-wing prescription that only cuts to wages and social spending, for example, can restore the rate of profit, and therefore the prosperity of the economy.

It is important that Marxist analysis does not lead to a counsel of despair in the circumstances of the present. To begin with, Marx showed that there are in fact a number of mechanisms which can restore profitability to a capitalist economy, even though a squeeze on workers' living standards appears as the most obvious to employers. Keynesian policies provide a practical antidote to the kneejerk of austerity. State-led infrastructure investments, for example, provide employment immediately, and through the multiplier effect, act as a stimulus to the whole economy. This kind of investment can provide the basis for a rise in productivity, supporting a new wave of investment and growth, or accumulation from capital's point of view. It is also the case that state investment, which requires only a return upon interest, acts to restore the average rate of profit in the rest of the economy.[108]

For Keynesians, the problems end there, and the prospects of harmonious economic growth open up, but Marx showed that the contradictory movements of capital accumulation will produce a new crisis out of the solutions to the old crisis. Countervailing pressures will already be at work, even as the rate of profit is restored, and the very remedies that stabilised the system beforehand, will now appear to capital as impediments to further growth. The confidence of capital will fall, and strident demands will be made on any government to improve conditions for profitability.

Moreover, many forms of investment, such as advancements in technology, particularly in the present, may lead to downward pressures on employment, with consequent deflationary effects on demand. It has become increasingly difficult in the post-war period to make progressive Keynesian policies effective in restoring capitalist growth. As a result, the pressure to reverse a reformist government's progressive direction in economic policy in the present will be immense. An understanding of the contradictions of capitalism, going beyond Keynesian prescriptions, will be essential in defending the interests of the working class at this point.

Yet again, despite the inherent difficulties, to disdain the pursuit of reformist governments, which would necessarily rely to an extent on some form of Keynesian policy programme, would be to fall into sectarianism, and the pursuit of revolutionary purity for its own sake. Equally, however, to imagine that electing a reformist government, however principled its party leaders appear to be, will provide a platform of power over capital, would be naïve. Time and again, reformist leaderships retreat or even collapse in the face of pressure from the institutions of the state, and the representatives of capital in industry and finance. The objective pressures of international markets provide reasons to bow to the interests of capital; armed only with Keynesian theory, the confidence of capital will always weigh heavily on reformist ministers.

This is not to say that nothing can be accomplished outside an actually revolutionary situation. The only force that can provide a counterbalance to the power of capital is that of an organised working class. If, however, the organisations of the proletariat lack autonomy from, or are overly dependent upon, the reformist project, then retreat, compromise and eventual defeat are the likely outcomes, even during the historically most favourable situations, such as Britain in 1945. The pressure of the movement is absolutely necessary to push back against capital so that a reformist government can make advances. The election of such a government is the easiest part of the process; ensuring it carries out meaningful reforms to the system is the real fight.

The movement therefore needs an independent, revolutionary core, that understands the limitations of Keynesian policy and the nature of the enemies within the state, who will struggle tooth and nail against any measures which limit capital. This means not only the necessity of building the widest possible mass movement, independently of the reformist party, but also a self-consciously revolutionary organisation. This must be capable of both acting within the wider movement in the most constructive ways possible, and maintaining an outlook and strategy that lie beyond the reformist agenda. A reformist government will either end in defeat, and a generational retreat for the cause of labour, or be pushed forward by an independently acting socialist movement. At that point, it would have to move beyond the limits of Keynesian policy and therefore, necessarily, the limits of capitalism. Only then would more permanent advances come within our grasp.

Notes

1. See Michael Roberts, *The Long Depression: How It Happened, Why It Happened, and What Happens Next* (Chicago 2016).

2. See Larry Elliott, 'Heretics welcome! Economics needs a new Reformation,' *The Guardian*, 17th December 2017: https://www.theguardian.com/business/2017/dec/17/heretics-welcome-economics-needs-a-new-reformation. Last accessed 22/5/18.

3. Larry Elliott, 'Slow economic growth is not the new normal, it's the old norm,' *The Guardian*, 30th July 2017: https://www.theguardian.com/business/2017/jul/30/slow-economic-growth-gdp-old-norm. Last accessed 22/5/18.

4. James K. Galbraith, *The End of Normal: The Great Crisis and the Future of Growth* (London 2014), p.67. With the image of 'freshwater and saltwater economists', p.70, Galbraith is referencing the argument of fellow economist Ricardo J. Caballero.

5. Ibid. p.68.

6. Steve Keen, *Debunking Economics: The Naked Emperor Dethroned?* (London 2011), p.17.

7. The French actually got around this problem in 1923, during the occupation of the Ruhr, by simply appropriating commodities like coal, and giving them over to French industry, thereby forcing Germany to pay reparations, 'in kind'.

8. John Maynard Keynes, *The General Theory of Employment, Interest and Money* in *The Essential Keynes*, ed. Robert Skidelsky (London 2015), pp.241-2.

9. Skidelsky, *Essential Keynes*, p.xxix, p.240.

10. Keynes, 'The End of Laissez-faire', in *Essential Keynes*, p.53.

11. Keynes, 'My Early Beliefs' (1938), in *Essential Keynes*, p.21.

12. For a discussion of the precise definitions and distinction between the two concepts see Geoff Mann, *In The Long Run We Are All Dead: Keynesianism, Political Economy and Revolution* (London 2017), pp.244-5.

13. Roberts, *The Long Depression*, p.277.

14. Skidelsky, *Essential Keynes*, p.7.

15. Keynes, 'My Early Beliefs', p.15 and p.19.

16. Ibid. p.21.

17. Ibid. p.22.

18. Keynes, 'Thomas Robert Malthus' (1933), in *Essential Keynes*, p.494. Skidelsky quotes Keynes as saying that it would have been better if economics had proceeded from Malthus than Ricardo; 'what a much wiser and richer place the world would be to-day!', p.490.

19. David Harvey, *Marx, Capital and the Madness of Economic Reason* (London 2017), p.5. To see Keynes as this kind of empiricist is not to contradict his depiction as an ethical idealist above; it is in fact characteristic of liberal empiricism to be reductively materialist at one level of analysis, only to lurch into abstract idealism at another.

20. Keynes, 'Malthus', p.495.

21. Ibid. p.502.

22. Keynes, 'The General Theory of Employment, Interest and Money' in *Essential Keynes*, p.256.

23. Keynes, 'Malthus', pp.494-5.

24. In 'Paying for the War', in *Essential Keynes*, pp.408, 412, Keynes argues that the 'increased earnings of the working class will not have benefited them one penny, but will have escaped through higher prices and higher profits'. Wage restraint is the answer in this situation. Keynes may be technically correct in this, taken over the long term, but people's lives happen in the immediate term also, and a rise in wages *now* will at least temporarily improve workers' standard of living. If in the longer

term, such gains tend to be eroded, this points to the fundamental injustices of the system, but also to the unrelenting nature of the class struggle within capitalism.

25. Keynes, 'The Economic Consequences of the Peace', p.33.

26. Ibid. p.99.

27. Ibid. p.100.

28. John Kenneth Galbraith, *The World Economy Since the Wars* (London 1994), p.80.

29. For example, 'Say's law: supply creates its own demand', *The Economist*, August 10th 2017: https://www.economist.com/economics-brief/2017/08/10/says-law-supply-creates-its-own-demand. Last accessed 22/5/18.

30. Karl Marx, *Theories of Surplus Value* (London: Lawrence and Wishart 1969), Part 2, Ch.17, p.501; and 'insipidities', Karl Marx, *Capital* (Moscow 1961), vol. 1, p.113 p.440n; vol. 3, pp.818-19, the 'thoughtless' Say resolves that the 'entire gross output' resolves itself into wages, profit and rent, ignoring the replacement of constant capital, 'which can never be transformed into revenue.' This is to say that as soon as the necessity of the reproduction of capital is taken into account, Say's Law is rendered invalid. Say, according to Marx, proceeds exclusively in his analysis from the point of view of the capitalist, rather from society as a whole, and his errors and 'insipidities' arise as a result.

31. Marx, *Capital* I, pp.113-14.

32. Keynes, 'General Theory', *Essential Keynes*, p.229.

33. Ibid. p.188.

34. Ibid. p.216.

35. Ibid. p.201.

36. Ibid. p.201.

37. Ibid. p.226.

38. Ibid. p.227.

39. Skidelsky, *Essential Keynes*, p.182.

40. Keynes, 'General Theory', p.227.

41. Ibid. p.246; and see Skidelsky's comment that

'faced with irreducible uncertainty, hoarding is more rational than investing', which means that under normal circumstances, private investment will fail to use fully the 'available human and technical resources' that would lead to full employment; p.183. In this argument, the more advanced the economy, the more that substantial unemployment will be a permanent feature.

42. Joan Robinson, *Economic Philosophy* (Harmondsworth 1962), pp.88-89.

43. See David Harvey, *Marx, Capital*.

44. Keynes, 'General Theory', pp.213-14.

45. David Harvey, *A Companion to Marx's Capital* (London 2013), vol. 2, p.217.

46. See Harvey's discussions in *Companion to Marx's Capital*, vol. 2, chs. 5-7, and for the relationship of fictitious capital to crisis, see p.181.

47. Keen, *Debunking Economics*, pp.327-28.

48. Ibid. pp.328-9.

49. Keynes, 'A Treatise on Money', in *Essential Keynes*, p.138.

50. Robert J Barbera, preface to Hyman Minsky, *John Maynard Keynes* (New York 1975), p.x.

51. Minsky, *John Maynard Keynes*, p.59.

52. Keynes, 'General Theory', p.256

53. Ibid. p.189.

54. Harvey, *Companion to Marx's Capital*, vol. 2, p.25, p.57, and p.306.

55. Rosa Luxemburg, 'The Accumulation of Capital: A Contribution to the Economic Theory of Imperialism' in *The Complete Works of Rosa Luxemburg, Volume II: Economic Writings 2* (London 2015), pp.6-342; p.11.

56. See Tony Norfield, *The City: London and the Global Power of Finance* (London 2016), and also Harvey's analysis (note 41 above).

57. Harvey, *Companion to Capital*, vol. 2, pp.216-17.

58. Keynes, 'General Theory', p.198.

59. Ibid. p.199.

60. Minsky, *John Maynard Keynes*, p.158.

61. Ibid. p.144.

62. Ibid. p.145 and p.166. Minsky was arguing that conservative theory had come to dominate a debased Keynesianism-in-practice, arguing for 'a high-consumption, egalitarian regime' but does not provide any social mechanism, or political force which could bring about such a policy change.

63. Robinson, *Economic Philosophy*, p.36.

64. For a brilliant exposition of this, and the emergence of the law of value from a pre-capitalist to a capitalist economy, see Octavio Columbo, 'Simple Commodity Production and Value Theory in Late Feudalism', in *Studies on Pre-Capitalist Modes of Production*, eds. Laura da Graca and Andrea Zingarelli (Leiden/Chicago 2015/16), pp.237-67.

65. Harvey, *Marx, Capital*, p.5.

66. To paraphrase E. P. Thompson, *The Making of the English Working Class* (London 1963), p.8.

67. Robinson, *Economic Philosophy*, p.47.

68. Harvey, *Marx, Capital*, p.144.

69. Ibid. p.5.

70. Ibid. p.5.

71. Robinson, *An Essay on Marxian Economics* (London 1942), p.xxi.

72. See above, part 1, p.4.

73. Robinson, *Marxian Economics*, pp.ix-x fails to distinguish the social tendency for prices to average around values, from the value to price proportions of particular commodities.

74. Harvey, *Marx, Capital*, pp.34-5.

75. Robinson, *Marxian Economics*, pp.26-7.

76. Steve Keen's attack on Marx's labour theory of value fails on many of the same grounds as does Robinson's, not least because he proceeds from Robinson's assumptions; Keen, *Debunking Economics*, p.423 and p.427, appears to simplify Robinson's argument, producing the entirely erroneous claim that Marx always supposed the rate of

surplus value to be constant; see Robinson, *Marxian Economics*, p.38, where she refers to it as the rate of exploitation. Keen in general is enthusiastic about the 'neo-Ricardian' economist Piero Sraffa, whose theories, Harvey explains, were used 'to destroy the prevailing (non-dialectical) notion of value theory in Marx', *Companion to Marx's Capital*, vol. 2, p.331, note 9. The version of value theory being defended here is the dialectical one.

77. Robinson, *Marxian Economics*, p.85; see above n.25, and Harvey, *Companion to Capital*, vol. 2, p.40.

78. Robinson, *Marxian Economics*, p.xii.

79. The failure to understand this seems to lie behind Steve Keen's rejection of labour as the source of surplus value; *Debunking Economics*, p.442. What both Keen and Robinson also fail to notice is that the labour theory of value is about the production of surplus value within capitalism, not the existence of nature's 'free gifts', for example; see John Bellamy Foster, *Marx's Ecology: Materialism and Nature* (New York 2000), particularly p.167.

80. For the most recent, and very effective, Marxist rebuttal of the transformation problem, discussed at the general level, see Michael Roberts, *Marx 200 – A review of Marx's economics 200 years after his birth* (Lulu.com 2018), pp.81-5.

81. Robinson, *Marxian Economics*, pp.36-8.

82. See Geert Reuten, 'The Productive Powers of Labour and the Redundant Transformation to Prices of Production: A Marx-immanent Critique and Reconstruction', *Historical Materialism* 25.3 (2017), pp.3-35; p.3; Reuten offers an interesting solution to the transformation problem itself, within Marx's own terms.

83. Robinson, *Marxian Economics*, p.ix, finds that the 'constant rate of exploitation in Volume III [of *Capital*] is not explained', noticing therefore that in other parts of the argument the rate of surplus value does change, but

not appreciating the function of holding it constant for the purpose of the overall analysis.

84. Ibid. p.36.

85. Paul Mattick, *Marx and Keynes: The Limits of the Mixed Economy* (London 1971), p.43. Mattick goes onto explain how values turn into prices 'by way of competition, by the search for profits and extra-profits which constitutes the capitalist contribution and reaction to the increasing productivity of labor'. For a full explanation of this whole issue, see ibid. ch.4, 'Value and Price', pp.40-50.

86. Keen, *Debunking Economics*, p.429; Keen demands that Marx's argument can achieve a multiplicity of conclusions without varying the holding assumptions, and also assumes that the point of the transformation tables is to predict prices from values, in real terms, which was clearly not Marx's purpose in this fragment.

87. See Roberts, *The Long Depression*, chapter 4, pp.59-64.

88. On these episodes see Gwyn A. Williams, *The Merthyr Rising* (London 1978), and Mick Jenkins, *The General Strike of 1842* (London 1980).

89. John K. Galbraith, *World Economy*, p.122.

90. Paul Foot, *The Vote: How it was Won and How it was Undermined* (London 2005), p.312.

91. Ibid. p.322.

92. Tony Cliff and Donny Gluckstein, *The Labour Party: A Marxist History* (London 1988), pp.230-2.

93. Ibid. p.222.

94. Foot, *The Vote*, p.321.

95. Ibid. p.329.

96. Cliff and Gluckstein, *Labour Party*, p.233.

97. Ibid. p.242,

98. Ibid. p.244.

99. See John Newsinger, *The Blood Never Dried: A People's History of the British Empire* (London 2006), particularly pp.198-213.

100. Foot, *The Vote*, p.333.

101. Cliff and Gluckstein, *Labour Party*, p.240.

102. John K. Galbraith, *World Economy*, p.235.

103. Ibid. p.218.

104. Ibid. p.219.

105. Michael Kidron, *Capitalism and Theory* (London 1974), p.19.

106. John K. Galbraith, *The Good Society: The Humane Agenda* (London 1996), p.115.

107. Cliff and Gluckstein, *Labour Party*, p.226.

108. Harvey, *Companion to Capital*, vol. 2, p.250.

About the author

Dominic Alexander is a member of Counterfire, for which he is the book reviews editor. He is a member of Stop the War Coalition and is an anti-austerity activist in north London. He is a medieval historian, author of the book *Saints and Animals in the Middle Ages*, a social history of medieval wonder tales, and has also published on London's first recorded revolutionary, William Longbeard, and his rebellion of 1196.

Further reading

David Harvey, *A Companion to Marx's Capital*, volumes 1 and 2 (London 2010 and 2013)

David Harvey, *Marx, Capital and the Madness of Economic Reason* (London 2017)

Michael Kidron, *Capitalism and Theory* (London 1974)

Paul Mattick, *Marx and Keynes: The Limits of the Mixed Economy* (London 1971)

Tony Norfield, *The City: London and the Global Power of Finance* (London 2016)

Michael Roberts, *The Long Depression: How It Happened, Why It Happened, and What Happens Next* (Chicago 2016)

Michael Roberts, *Marx 200 – A review of Marx's economics 200 years after his birth* (Lulu.com 2018)

Help us remake socialist politics for the 21st century

Counterfire helps build the movements against war, austerity, racism and climate change.

Corbyn's victory has helped the left and we need to stay mobilised to support and defend him. We think fundamental change comes from below, and that socialists need to get organised to help make this happen. We want to see a left that can make a real difference to the world, and we are growing.

Counterfire.org is one of the best-read websites on the radical left, and we are now producing a regular free tabloid in the same spirit. We have Counterfire groups across the country and they need your help and ideas to make change happen.

Help remake socialist politics for the twenty-first century. Join us, we are stronger together.

www.counterfire.org/join